Got Cancer?
Congratulations!

...now you can start living

- Life After Diagnosis
- Resources & Remedies
- Alternative Approaches
- Decisions Only You Can Make

- Frequently Asked Questions About Cancer
- How To Transition to a Healthy Lifestyle
- Spiritual Aspects of Healing
- Disease Prevention

By

Surina Ann Jordan

Foreword by Dr. Emerson E. Harrison, M.D.

Preface by Alton B. Pollard, III, Ph.D.

ISBN: 1-4107-8933-0 (e-book)
ISBN: 1-4107-8932-2 (Paperback)

This book is printed on acid free paper.

Body Temple Publishing
P.O. Box 23854
Baltimore, Maryland 21203

1stBooks – rev. 03/28/05

This book is not a medical publication and is in no way attempting to provide medical advice, prescription or treatment. It is written for the purposes of education and inspiration. It contains many helpful suggestions. The author of this book recommends you seek a qualified health practitioner.

Acknowledgements

A special thanks to JoAnn Branch, Jessica Pollard, Calvin Jackson Vivian Connor and Gerri Pinkett for the time you so willingly gave to complete this work.

Thank you **Reverend Glen Wallace** for the prayer and encouragement to do this work.

Thanks to the Coleman, Pinkett, Portlock, Petty, Turner, Jordan, Daniel, Bayton and Glen families for your love.

Thanks to my hero and soul mate, **Herbert Jordan III** for truly you are my good and perfect gift. Thanks to **Princess Roxane**, our wonderful daughter.

Dedications – To Our Support Team:

Barbara Pembamoto

Mom Jordan, Dad & Mom Coleman

Joyce & Frank Petty

Pat Troy Brooks

Dr. Mark Lomax

Gerri & Gilbert Pinkett

Terry & Carol Brown

Mary & Terek Green

Joe & Marijane Lawson

The Usama Family

In memory of loved ones who would have been soldiers if they had only known what they were fighting and what weapons were available:

Jackie Portlock	Rusty James
Richard Wynder	Johnny Rogers
Herman Palmer	Lee Worth
Hilton Palmer	Hattie Mae Palmer
Harrison Hopkins	Mary Meekins
Joan Coursey	

To the Creator, the source of my very existence...

I love you.

Table of Contents

Foreword

One afternoon, seven years ago, Herbert Jordan was an emergency patient who was sent to me by a colleague. My colleague's sense of urgency was that he had never seen a prostate in a young man in such condition. I will never forget the guy who had become known throughout the Emory Medical System as the guy with the "melon size" prostate. How he was able to function under the circumstance was not clear.

The weeks ensued and I worked with a team of other specialists and the diagnosis was a rare case of Non-Hodgkins Lymphoma (lymphatic cancer).

I observed that Mr. Jordan and his family had an interesting approach to life. Their diet contained little processed foods. Their disposition was calm. They were respectful but well informed and always open to additional information in order to make the decision that was right for them. Studies show that patients that have hope and a passion for life are the best partners a doctor can have. The attitude and circumstance in which the individual lives is a large factor.

This book is about personal responsibility in the midst of a health crisis. It defines the patient's role and the doctor's role. It brings focus and suggests a set of prioritized next steps. It provides information and offers the encouragement you will need during your healing period.

This book will prove to be very resourceful to patients and their families. All readers will benefit in that much of what is presented are ideas that will not only help during cancer treatment but also help prevent cancer and other diseases.

Dr. Emerson E. Harrison, M.D.
Atlanta Urological Consultants, P.C.

Preface

When Jesus came out of the wilderness, the biblical record states, "he returned in the power of the Spirit of Galilee" and shortly thereafter went into his own hometown of Nazareth, and the lesson says again, "as was his custom" he went to the temple. In honor of his homecoming the resident rabbi asked this traveler who had come home if he would read the message for the day. He passed him the scroll and Jesus unrolled it until he found the place wherein it is written in the Hebrew Scriptures, in the book of the prophet Isaiah, "The Spirit of the Lord is upon me." (Luke 4:16-20).

I am reminded of Jesus' first sermon, the initial proclamation of the unfolding meaning of his life and work, after reading the wise words that Surina Jordan shares with us in these pages. Hers in a slender volume but no more needed to be said. After all, how many words did Jesus himself write down? Surina's life is her witness. She has taken fully to heart Jesus' mandate to declare the good news, to heal the broken-hearted, to proclaim deliverance and recovery, to set at liberty and, she tells us, the acceptable year is now.

These are difficult days. All around us people are dying, the dead of defeat, despair, distress, indifference, discrimination, mis-education, misdiagnosis, disbelief, diseases, despondency, drugs, drink, poor diet, false doctrine, addictions, dependencies and devastations of every description. The enemy of life is everywhere, and the word of the Lord that comes to us through our sister Surina is to rejoice and embrace our health - spiritual, physical, mental, medical, economic, political, educational, divine, godly health.

Surina Ann Jordan's book is a gift of love to us. Her words inspire and inform, reminding us that ours is the God-given responsibility to live life more holistically and abundantly. Surina offers practical and helpful suggestions to show us how. The opportunity is ours to act in faith.

Alton B. Pollard, III, Ph.D.
Director, Program of Black Church Studies and
Associate Professor of Religion and Culture
Candler School of Theology at Emory University

Introduction

Who would title a book Got Cancer? Congratulations! What on earth was she thinking? Let me explain. Being diagnosed with cancer is the ultimate wakeup call. It is shocking yet personal. You feel violated and frightened. You come face to face with the fact that lifestyle and poor decisions have possibly gotten you into this situation.

And now from this moment you have the opportunity to start reversing, healing and preventing the recurrence of the disease! There are still choices to be made and a new life to begin. Whether you have two months or ten years, this book will encourage you and suggest where you can start. Congratulations! Now you can really start living.

As of this writing, it is estimated that one out of three Americans will be diagnosed with cancer. If you were to make a list of the people you know that have been diagnosed with cancer, those still living and those who have died, the number would be overwhelming. According to the American Cancer Society more than 1.2 million people will be diagnosed with cancer this year. Some 1500 people lose their lives from cancer every day!

It is also unfortunate that with all of our modern medicine and technology, we have not been able to reduce the number nor stop the increase in cases. Conventional treatment of cancer has for the most part remained the same for over 20 years. Many of us die from cancer treatments, which is primarily using poison to fight poison or cut and burn methods. No significant progress has been made in discovering a cure for cancer. There is a standard treatment and as a result, some of us make it and some of us do not.

In my humble opinion, there is no real mystery about cancer and many other diseases. The most shocking statistic is one that conventional and alternative medical industries agree upon and that is 80% of all disease in the U.S. is preventable and is based on poor eating and lifestyle.

Doctors are to be respected, but they are not God. Doctors are your partners and they know what they have been taught. However, few medical schools in this country require any course work in the area of nutrition or alternative medicine. Doctors, like anyone else, will not recommend something, of which they are not knowledgeable. On the other hand doctors have little demonstrable evidence that patients are willing to make lifestyle changes. As a result, there is little encouragement from your doctor for using alternatives or nutrition for healing. My suggestion is that you never give up your rights when making decisions regarding your health.

My husband Herb and I had to make these decisions, when he was diagnosed with Non-Hodgkins Lymphoma. This is cancer of the lymphatic system. We always referred to his condition as a diagnosis. To say "I have cancer" or "my cancer" would be activating the wrong message about your state of health. This type of intimate ownership is akin to putting out the welcome mat for cancer to take up permanent residence with in your body.

And seven years later, we're walking in his healing. Thank God!

Our prayer for you is that you seek God, wise council, and then make your own decisions.

The Spiritual Nature of This Book

I am proud to be a Christian, inspired to do the work of our Creator, even though I have observed being a Christian means different things to different people.

For example, many of us confess Jesus and accept Him into our hearts. However, we have done little to strengthen that relationship.

We lack discipline, treat Jesus like a puppet, don't want to learn or to be taught, make our own decisions independent of Christ and listen to the wrong voices. I call it "salvation station". Salvation station is where Christianity 101 is taught and hopefully mastered. Many of us refuse to leave that classroom. As a result, we are under achievers, living life according to what we "think" we should be doing. The true map is the path of personal growth and development. It is the testament of God's will and purpose for our lives. Christ becomes our holistic coach for the spirit, mind, body and soul.

The holistic coach has credentials for living and wants access to every dimension of our lives everyday. He gives us a test after each teaching and helps us pass them. He is always with us. He's building character, patience and stewardship. He is preparing us to complete that special work planned just for each of us. It is not God's Will for us to be sick or diseased.

Although I am Christian my message transcends all denominations. You do not want to throw away this message. There is a spiritual dimension wherein all of us can agree. It is foundational and must be considered as we partake in our professed religion or denomination. It is within this space and time where we meet the Creator, The Great "I Am".

Who is the Creator? The Creator is the presence of love. The love of the Creator started before time and it is within time. He (or she) is on time and is already at the end of time. He is where you are, with you as you go and is there before you arrive. He is everywhere and in everything at the same time. Teachers can't teach him and scientists die trying to understand him. The creation of man and woman was the culmination of the physical and the spiritual. This love gave to us the ability to decide and make choices. This gift of choice will never be taken from us. We may choose to live in harmony with the Creator or attempt life without him. Catherine Ponder, author of **The Dynamic Laws of Healing,** suggests, "choosing life without the spirit of the Creator is the root of all sickness and disease" (Page 2).

Facing the Fears

Being told that you have cancer can be one of the most devastating things that can happen in life. All of a sudden, the biggest most challenging problem in your life no longer seems that big or pressing. The fear of suffering and death is prominent. And then comes the emotional roller coaster and fears; how and when will you tell your family. Who will raise the children? You may recall the suffering and death of a friend or loved one as a result of cancer. You envision that happening to you. Everyone is bio-chemically similar but also very different, which makes no two experiences alike.

> *The truth of the matter is that none of us have more than the existing second of life available to us.*

The truth of the matter is that none of us have more than the existing second of life available to us. Death is just a reality that seems more pressing when diagnosed with cancer. However, many often outlive those of us who have not been diagnosed with cancer.

So be encouraged, relax your mind and let's put this in perspective, so that we can develop your own strategy to do battle. The good news is that cancer is a health crisis not a death sentence, but you are in for the fight of your life.

> *The good news is that cancer is a health crisis not a death sentence.*

Hopefully, by the time you have completed this book or have read the relevant chapters, a lot of the mystery about your diagnosis will be clear. Know that information is power. The more you learn the less fear you will experience.

There is a remnant of cancer survivors who have pushed back on the disease cycle of cancer and have made decisions about their approach and how best to deal with such a verdict. The following pages contain the alternative approaches and lifestyle changes many of them have made.

This information is for your consideration and is in no way a recommendation for treatment. I address lifestyle issues and ways of preventing sickness and disease. If you have been diagnosed with cancer, this book will help prepare you for battle by offering strategies for living in the midst of the fight. It will also help you to think clearly about the decisions you must make.

What *is* in this book:

Within this book you will come face to face with some hard truths. No blame, no guilt, just truth. On the other hand it also initiates love, a call to action and correction.

This book provides a high-level summary of information about cancer. It attempts to remove the panic and calm the fear and stress, which comes with a diagnosis such as cancer. It provides the path for you to reconcile where you are so you can move forward. I discuss the state of conventional treatments and things you may not have known about alternative treatment.

I attempt to provide answers to "What an individual's options are when they are diagnosed with cancer?" I present sources for alternative care centers, and remedies, which one might choose to pursue. I address how to use food, herbs and nature to improve your health. Also the natural approaches to deal with the side effects of conventional cancer treatments are discussed.

What *is not* in this book:

Although this book is comprehensive in its intended purpose of providing viable alternatives to conventional medicine, I do not include the details of conventional treatments because this information is readily available. This book emphasizes the alternatives and how to live a healthy lifestyle.

Good health is not a gift, it is a lifestyle.

In Love and Good Health,

Surina Ann Jordan

Chapter 1

What You Need To Know About Cancer?

Chapter 1

What You Need To Know About Cancer?

What is cancer?

What is cancer? Cancer is a disease caused by a breakdown in the body's ability to destroy or limit the growth of abnormal cells. Cancer cells are renegades, which have broken away from the body's radar and are no longer detected and destroyed. The body no longer has the ability to control the mechanism of cell replication. These cells then multiply so fast, that large amounts of them form a mass in the weakest or most vulnerable part of the body. These masses are called malignant tumors. The most challenging part about cancer is that these cells have access to the entire blood stream and can spread and develop tumors in other parts of the body. Cancer cells continue to divide and form more cancer cells. These cells are radical and are no longer being controlled or destroyed by the brain and the normal immune response within the body. Everyone has a degree of abnormal cell growth but a fit immune system is able to destroy or reprogram these cells into normal cells and life goes on.

However, in the case where the body has been weakened and the immune system has been compromised, the opportunity is provided for these abnormal cells to grow rapidly and destroy the good cells in the process. If left undetected these cells become parasitic, draining the body of energy and nutrients that are needed for repair. These cells weaken the body and drain more and more energy. Once this disease is in progress, it can go undetected for years, according to the American Institute for Cancer Research.

Every cell in the body has the potential to become cancerous.

Every cell has the potential to become cancerous. A cell may either be supported by the body to remain healthy or it can be weakened and become abnormal. What causes the abnormal cell growth? The debate among scientists continues. However there has been major progress in this area. The following are known promoters of abnormal cell growth:

1. suppressing the body's natural cleansing/detoxification process
2. diet and malnutrition

3

3. stress and psychological factors

4. environmental factors

5. obesity

6. genetics

Factors That Cause Abnormal Cell Growth

1. Suppressing the body's Natural Cleansing & Detoxification Process

The body attempts to rid itself of toxins and excessive mucus and other waste. This process is often mistaken as a common cold. The body eliminates waste through various locations of the body. It is a natural (but for many an embarrassing) process. Instead of letting it take its course, we often get an over the counter drug to dry it up. This drying up, forces the toxins back into the blood stream and they settle somewhere else in the body. The body's next attempt to rid itself of waste may surface as what appears to be the flu. This time the excretions are accompanied by aches and pains. We may take something to suppress it again. The next time, it may surface as bronchitis and then the next time pneumonia. Meanwhile it is weakening the immune system. Over the years this process is the start of degenerative disease in the body, normally attacking the weakest organ or area of the body (Yozwick 116).

2. Diet And Malnutrition

The lack of whole foods, fiber, fresh fruits and vegetables is a major factor in our inability to prevent disease. Consumption of over processed foods and fats from animal protein are high on the list of inferior foods. These foods and the addition of caffeine, alcohol and cigarettes are known to strip the body of key nutrients causing major deficiencies in the body.

While the U.S. is abundant in vegetables and fruits, less than 10 percent of Americans consume the five-plus servings of fruits and vegetables needed each day to get enough of these nutrients. And our intake of vitamin E-rich grains, nuts, and seeds is also low. Studies show that almost 50 percent of Americans between the ages of 19 and 50 consume less than 70 percent of the recommended amount.

We must also reduce animal protein intake. Americans consume four times the amount of protein needed on a daily basis. This excessive amount of protein causes the kidneys to work harder, and strips the body of much needed minerals like calcium and magnesium. It increases the acidity in the body, causes diseases in the colon and weakens the immune system. Fifty-five percent of the antibiotics produced in the United States are fed to livestock. We then ingest these antibiotics, which weakens our immune systems.

3. Stress and Psychological Factors

A healthy state of mind with limited stress is also important for a healthy lifestyle. We cannot control the amount of stressors that we encounter on a day-to-day basis. Many have occupations that are high stress by nature however, we must avoid chronic (mental and emotional) stressors, worries and fears.

University of Wisconsin-Madison psychologist Christopher Coe has found that "Life's stressful events seem to reach all the way to the immune system, and weaken our ability to battle illness." Stress can alter the chemical makeup in the body, once that happens the body becomes more vulnerable for disease. According to Leon Chaitow, N.D., D.O. of London, England, " when the stress is too severe, or if it becomes chronic", for example the loss of a loved one, divorce or separation, "chemical changes begin to occur in the body, creating an environment which may increase the risk of serious disease, including cancer."

4. Environmental Factors

Overall Chemical Exposure

In any given day, we are exposed to chemicals in our drinking water and the air we breathe. Our food is grown and sprayed with pesticides. Our food is processed with colorings and additives. Our cosmetics and beauty products are laced with harmful chemicals. Over time all these chemicals contribute to the weakening of the immune system.

Carcinogenic Toxins

It is important to avoid long or frequent exposure to carcinogenic chemicals and contaminants found in everyday household items. Solvents, furniture polishes, cleaning fluids, detergents, paint thinners, pesticides, garden and lawn chemicals, paints, air fresheners, all contain carcinogenic chemicals. It may not be one particular item, but a combination that causes a toxic situation.

The health food store has multipurpose soaps and cleansers that are more friendly to the body. Also, if cleanup to the tub or sink takes place right away instead of allowing the dirt to buildup, mild hand soap and a sponge will do.

A tightly sealed house with little ventilation is a known problem as well. Studies have shown that the air quality in many of our homes is three times more toxic than the air outside. It could take weeks for these chemicals to break down. Air the house out at least once each week. Also avoid smog, car fumes, factory exhausts and if possible cigarette -filled places.

Exposure to Electromagnetic Fields

Avoid living or working in areas with close proximity to power lines and generating stations. Also do not sleep near electric devices such as blankets, waterbeds and even clock radios that are to close to the head. Avoid constant use of one piece cellular phones.

Smoking

Cigarettes are carcinogens. Smokers are 20-30 times more likely to develop cancer than non-smokers. A recent article in the Health Scout News indicated that smokers not only have to be concerned about the long-term effects of smoking like lung cancer and heart disease but studies have shown that every cigarette affects the body immediately.

Smoking deprives the body of oxygen and all cells need oxygen. Smoking weakens muscles and increases bone loss. In smokers the injury rate increases and it takes longer for wounds to heal. Some refer to smoking as "legal suicide". The only uncertainty is how disease will be manifested.

Alcohol

Alcohol is a poison. When you drink, the entire body is put on red alert. Little attention is given to anything else but ridding the body of this invader. The sleepiness and loss of consciousness, and vomiting is the body's attempt to save and rid itself from this poison. Alcohol kills brain cells, weakens the liver and weakens the immune system.

5. Obesity

An over-weight, malnourished body can lead to cancer and other diseases. Michael Fumento, author of, **The Fat of the Land,** is a medical journalist and a resident fellow at the American Enterprise Institute. Fumento provides insightful arguments regarding obesity in the U.S. as an epidemic. According to Fumento, obesity kills over 300,000 Americans a year! One of the main dangers associated with obesity is that many of us are not aware. Society recognizes symptoms (or the ailments suffered) but not the cause.

Overeating puts the body at risk of disease. Obesity is typically brought on by the constant consumption of large volumes of inferior foods. Inferior foods are processed, high in saturated fats and refined (white) sugar.

Being overweight taxes the skeletal structure and the major organs causing them to work harder with fewer nutrients. Being overweight is accompanied by irregularity in the bowels and poor elimination of toxins.

6. Genetics

Many feel that they are predisposed to have certain types of diseases due to their family's medical history. For many the future state of health looks bleak. Our family history may indicate a high instance of high blood pressure, diabetes and cancer. Genetically the cards are stacked against them. Many have assumed that these diseases for them are inevitable.

There is good news! Genetics is only part of the cause of these diseases. Unhealthy living and bad habits often trigger cancer. Our genetic blueprint indicates that we have strengths and weaknesses in certain areas, which makes us more or less vulnerable to certain diseases. However we all have the ability to prevent the occurrence of these diseases by living a lifestyle of prevention. Unless there is a spark of fire, a forest fire can never happen. Unhealthy living and bad habits are the sparks that fuel the genetic fire.

Life Extension vs Quality of Life

In a general discussion about the treatment of cancer, we will look at the conventional vs alternative approaches for cures.

Barry Lynes in his book, **The Healing of Cancer**, in a discussion on the effects of chemotherapy, radiation and surgery suggests that as cures, these treatments are suspect. As early as 1969, Hardin Jones, Ph.D., a professor of medical physics and physiology at the University of California, Berkeley, stated that according to his research statistics, the cancer patient who received no treatment had a greater life expectancy than the one who received treatment:

"For a typical type of cancer, people who refused treatment live an average of twelve and a half years. Those who accepted surgery and other kinds of treatment lived an average of only three years. I attribute this to the traumatic effect of surgery on the body's natural defense mechanism. The body has a natural kind of defense against every type of cancer" (page 8).

The side effects of traditional (conventional) treatments can be devastating and can cause more suffering then the disease itself. Many people have no pain prior to treatment. For example, if the doctor gives you 6 months to live, how would you like to spend that time? You could go the conventional route and spend the time suffering from nausea, joint aches & pains, depression, fevers, no energy while potentially accelerating your illness. Or you could choose to live 6 (or more) months really living!

Bad cells need food also. If you cut off the food source of the cancer cells; provide the body with more energy by embracing some of the living principles in this book, you could experience the most meaningful chapter of your life. It could be the best

13

part of your entire life. You could spend the time appreciating family, friends and nature. It is also highly possible that six months will turn into a year, 2 years, 10 years or more! This decision is yours to make.

My husband for example, chose some chemotherapy, no surgery and no radiation. Now we are actively living the principles for prevention and maintenance to prevent recurrence of the disease.

Whatever you decide, I implore you to become your primary caregiver. Most doctors see a certain number of patients a day and may not have the time or full knowledge of your situation. Don't take it personally. Make sure to practice what needs to be said to the doctor within a small amount of time. Don't assume that your doctor remembers anything about your case from your last visit or phone call. Don't assume he remembers the medication he has previously prescribed or any allergies you might have. It is a good idea to make a list of questions. Figure 1.1 provides a sample list of questions that will assist you with your initial visit after you have been diagnosed with cancer.

Handling brief doctor's visits can be difficult and is another reason why we must manage our own health. Allow doctors to become one of several resources in our approach to living a healthy lifestyle.

Figure 1.1 - Questions for Your Doctor About Your Diagnosis

1. What is the complete diagnosis?

2. How was the diagnosis determined, what test?

3. What stage is the cancer?

4. What is the best case scenario?

5. What is the worse case scenario?

6. What are his or her recommended next steps?

7. What team of doctors do you work with on these type of cases?

8. Have you had patients with this type of diagnosis before?

9. What path did they take?

10. Where are the best oncologists (in the area)? What makes him/her the best?

11. Off the record question, if this were your Mom or Dad, what treatment would you recommend to them?

12. What alternative treatment is available with cases like mine?

13. I would like to get a second opinion. Who would you recommend?

14. What are the side effects of the recommended treatment?

15. Since you consider 5 years cancer-free a cure, what side effects of the recommended treatment will surface after 5 years?

16. Is this treatment experimental? What is the survival rate for others who have taken this treatment?

Notes:

_____

_____

_____

_____

_____

Chapter 1 - Summary/What You Need To Know About Cancer

- Cancer is the growth of abnormal cells that the body no longer controls.

- There are several known factors that cause cancer:
  - Suppressing the body's Natural Cleansing/Detoxification Process – Let the body clean itself
  - Diet And Malnutrition – many illnesses are accelerated due to malnutrition
  - Stress and Psychological Factors – Stress must be managed
  - Environmental Factors – Some we control others we cannot
  - Obesity – Being overweight causes health problems
  - Genetics – Don't have the final say; lifestyle is key

- Quality of life vs. life extension must be considered when approaching treatment for cancer.

- You must become your own primary caregiver.

- Preparing for your doctor's visit is key.

Chapter 2

What Are Some Treatment Options

Chapter 2

What Are Some Treatment Options

For some of us, many alternative treatments are cost prohibitive. However, the thing to keep in mind is that we must starve abnormal cells to prevent them from increasing. With the proper food and other lifestyle changes, this can be accomplished with fewer dollars and side effects from traditional medicine.

Many in the medical field see cancer as a crisis that requires radical treatments that in many cases are disruptive to the natural flow of healing in the body. Alternative approaches are vast and varied. Most of the alternative approaches have a basic underlying premise, which is *do the body no harm*. As a result, every approach appears to have some good, however some are more effective than others.

What we cannot under estimate is the value of a support system and a peaceful environment in which to launch your healing strategy. This is addressed in chapter 3 entitled Next Steps.

Conventional Medicine

A Discussion of Primary Treatments

In most states, medical doctors are required to administer 1 of 3 treatments to cancer patients and many times, a combination of the three. These treatments are not cures, but rather attempts to extend life. They are also the treatments that often damage the body beyond repair. Know that surviving 5 years after diagnosis is considered a cure according to the National Cancer Institute.

> *... If the approach to treatment is only 5 years, then life beyond that time is not considered.*

Therefore if the approach to treatment is only 5 years, then life beyond that time is not considered. You should also know that one of the long-term side effects of these treatments is cancer.

This approach treats the symptom and rarely addresses the cause of the problem. Prior to treatment, the stage of the disease must be determined. Staging involves tests to learn the extent of the cancer. That is whether the disease has spread from the original site to other areas in the body. If the cancer has spread to other areas within the body, it is called metastasis. It is important to know the stage of the disease in order to plan the best treatment. For example, in stage one the malignancy is considered isolated and is more treatable.

Stage IV however, is advanced cancer. The cancer has metastasized. Treatment at this stage, in conventional medicine, is for life extension and mostly experimental. The short-term side effects can be devastating. In Stage II the tumors are typically into the muscle wall and stage III involves the lymph nodes.

Before you can make a decision regarding treatment you will need to gather information from your team of physicians. A list of questions have been prepared for you (see figure 1.1 in chapter one) to assist with gathering this information. You may have other questions specific to your condition. If so add them to the list. Make sure you write the answers down. This is your baseline. You should expect improvement towards remission/cure with each treatment.

In conventional medicine, surgery, chemotherapy and radiation therapy are standard treatments according to the National Cancer Institute. Let's discuss them and others briefly.

Surgery

Often times surgery is used when there is a malignant mass in the body that is considered removable without an immediate threat. The removal of certain malignancies may require organs to be removed, for example, the removal of a kidney, lung, or for men, the prostate gland. This type of surgery can impact the quality of your life permanently. However, if you feel your choice is based on survival, having this type of surgery may be a small price to pay.

Chemotherapy

Chemotherapy is the treatment of cancer cells with one or more very powerful pharmaceuticals.

The major objection to "chemo" is that these drugs do not discriminate between normal and cancerous cells, but attacks all rapidly dividing cells. Destroying good cells and the body's reaction to being poisoned is what causes the side effects of chemotherapy. It also weakens the already taxed immune system.

I am not here to convince you to take chemo or not to take chemo. It is to give you enough information so that you can make the decision. If you decide to have chemotherapy there will be side effects. See the chapter four for questions on side effects.

Radiation Therapy

Radiation is used as a treatment for several different conditions. Sometimes a malignant tumor can be too large to remove. Radiation may be used to reduce the size of the tumor prior to surgery. This reduces certain risks associated with this type of surgery.

Radiation is also administered as a sweeper or as a tool to ensure that the area where the malignancy is located is treated at the microscopic level.

This is the use of high-energy radiation from x-rays, gamma rays, neutrons, and other sources to kill cancer cells and shrink tumors. Radiation may come from a machine outside the body (external-beam radiation therapy), or from materials called radioisotopes.

The side affects may include permanent damage to nearby organs and of course cancer itself.

Hormone Therapy

This treatment adds, blocks, or removes hormones. To slow or stop the growth of certain cancers (such as prostate and breast cancer), hormones may be given to block the body's natural hormones. Sometimes surgery is needed to remove the source of hormones (NCI, glossary).

Biological Therapy

Biological therapies use the body's immune system either directly or indirectly, to fight cancer or to lessen the side effects that may be caused by some cancer treatments. Biological therapies are designed to repair, stimulate, or enhance the immune system's responses (NCI, glossary).

Bone Marrow And Stem Cell Transplant

Bone marrow is a material within the bones. It creates red blood cells, which transports oxygen throughout the body. It produces white blood cells, which fight infections. It also produces platelets, which are the clotting mechanisms needed to stop bleeding.

Stem Cells are blood cells found in bone marrow or the blood stream that are in an early stage of development.

A compatible donor (usually a close relative) must be found. The treatment actually destroys the cells in your bone marrow using very high dosages of chemotherapy, and is then replaced by the "healthy cells" from your donor.

There is also a procedure called autologous transplant or an auto graft, which is when you can use your own bone marrow or stems cells. It is the same process as stated above except there is no donor. This is possible if the cancer has not spread to the bone.

Pharmaceuticals and Prescription Drugs

Pharmaceuticals and Prescription Drugs alter the state of the condition in the body. They do not cure or heal and are not without consequences. There is always a side effect. These drugs have been tested individually but are not always tested in relationship to other drugs. Make sure you understand what they are and decide for yourself if you can live with the consequence.

Alternative Therapy
Alternative Approaches To Consider

Any approach to healing outside of the traditional medical methods is considered alternative. Know that every alternative approach is not going to be best for you. But to ignore the entire world of alternatives is again like throwing the baby out with the bath water.

Naturopathy or Alternative therapy addresses the root cause of a disease or ailment. The approach is to do no harm, but to give the body what it needs to heal itself. This requires multi-dimensional care. This is very different from conventional medicine, which treats symptoms. After the "light bulb" in the body blows out is when conventional medicine is applied. What caused it to blow will not be addressed. Conventional medicine is also highly specialized. What I mean by this is that one physician only treats symptoms relating to the ear, nose and throat, another only deals with the feet, and another only the brain. For example, we know that a chronic ear infection in many cases is caused by a misaligned spine, having very little to do with the ear itself. Or that nausea can be the result of an overworked liver not a digestive issue.

Alternative therapy is an array of healing practices, including diet and clinical nutrition, homeopathy, acupuncture, herbal medicine, hydrotherapy, therapeutic exercise, spinal and soft-tissue manipulation, physical therapies involving electric currents, ultrasound, light therapy and therapeutic counseling. It is a system of medicine based on six basic principles:

1. **Employ the healing power of nature** - the body has the power to heal itself. The role of the naturopath is to facilitate this natural process.
2. **Treat the cause rather than the effect** - seek the underlying cause of a disease rather than simply suppressing the system.
3. **First, do no harm** - employ safe and effective nature therapies.
4. **Treat the whole person** - understand the individual's complex interaction of physical, mental, emotional, spiritual and social factors.
5. **Teach self healing** - a naturopath is a teacher, educating, empowering and motivating the patient to assume more personal

responsibility for their own wellness by adopting a healthy attitude, lifestyle and diet.

6. **Emphasize prevention** - Prevention of disease is best accomplished through dietary and lifestyle habits, which support health.

Alternative Cancer treatment covers a broad range of therapies. Many treatment centers may use a combination of approaches. These include detoxifications, immune-system enhancement, nutritional support, healthy diets, and bio-magnet therapy, along with such biological substances as hydrogen peroxide, ozone, laetrile, shark cartilage, and many others. After identifying which conditions in the patient manifest in illness, the naturopathic (or alternative medicine physician) advises the patient on the methods most appropriate for creating a return to health. In order to become free of illness, it is often necessary for the patient to make both dietary and lifestyle changes.

> *A permanent lifestyle change is what is needed in order to properly rid the body from disease.*

Many people with cancer want to be restored to the point where they were prior to having cancer. The problem with this thinking is that the lifestyle they were leading is what contributed to the cancer.

A permanent lifestyle change is what is needed in order to properly rid the body from disease and to help keep it healthy and functioning properly.

Chapter 2 – Summary/What Are Some Treatment Options

- Conventional Medical treatment of cancer consists primarily of chemotherapy, surgery and radiation.
- Conventional Medical treatment for cancer deals with life extension.
- Alternative treatments address the root cause of the disease.
- Alternative treatments provide a broad range of healing practices.
- A permanent lifestyle change is needed for good health.

Chapter 3

Next Steps – Principles For Living

Chapter 3

Next Steps - Principles For Living

It's time to do battle! Don't take this one lying down. I was told if you are in a fight and lose, make sure that your enemy remembers he was in a fight. Here are the Living Principles for your healing strategy:

1. **Stay In Love.**
2. **Tune Up Your Spirit (Identify the Enemy).**
3. **Develop A Lifestyle to Support Treatment and Wellness.**
4. **Make Key Decisions.**

Stay In Love

One of my struggles is remembering that if I love the Creator, then He expects me [His creation] to love me a lot more than I do. This kind of love is described in the Holy Bible. It starts with Psalms 139, which explains that before I was in my mother's womb, He [The Creator God] knew me and planned each day of my life before I started living. And then I think of Matthew 23:39 which states that we should love others as we love ourselves. It reminds me that it is impossible to really love someone if I don't love myself.

Being married has reinforced the fact that love is a verb. It is action oriented not a noun (thing). Love is something you do. It is therefore what I do that demonstrates my love for the Creator. It is what I do for me and to me that demonstrates my love for the Creator and myself. It is that special place in my heart that allows the Spirit of the Creator to remind me that "I am fearfully and wonderfully made". I see that my body is the temple of the Spirit of the Creator and I dare not defile it or I will destroy myself (I Corinthians 3:16).

It is in that expression of graditude to God for allowing me to be who I am that I find a relationship built on mutual admiration and love that surpasses human comprehension. "Now I see that how I love, care and treat me and how I allow others to treat me is an act of worship". It is a 24 hour seven day a week process that ensures a peaceful, holistic existence.

Surina Ann Jordan

It is that demonstration and respect for a wonderfully, predestined being, that is fully empowered to worship, praise and glorify the Creator, which governs my way of living. It is also a reminder that I am a spirit living out a physical existence, not a physical being living a spiritual existence. It is not what we do for God that is key. It is what God does through us.

> *It is not what we do for God that is key. It is what God does through us.*

My spirit, relationship with God and purpose are foundational for my life.

In Figure 3.1, The Pyramid for Holisitic Living, life starts with the existence of the Creator, the force from which all life flows. It is the **Love of the Creator.** As we become aware and begin to acknowledge the existence of the Creator and how essential he is to our lives, a relationship is formed. We develop appreciation and **Love for the Creator.** It is this foundation on which we operate in love and are in full alignment with him through Jesus the Christ. We can then appreciate self and its value. We then understand **Love of Self.** It is that self appreciation that allows us to be good stewards of our lives and our health. The critical

36

assignment (mentioned in Psalm 139), our divine purpose and passion, of which no one else can perform, can then be realized. Our value and meaning in life is then solidified. We then develop habits and seek knowledge and become good stewards that support our ability to fulfill that divine purpose. The extent and ability to demonstrate **Love for Others** is directly asscociated with that assignment. My divine purpose is the gift/expertise that others need.

Walking in Love, is key to being in good health.

Meditation

I love you Lord, I love you Lord,
for you are the source of my very existence and I love you Lord.
I need you Lord, you are the source of my very existence and I need you Lord.
I want you Lord, for you are the source of my very existence and I want you Lord
For you are the source of my very existence and I love you Lord.

Figure 3.1 - Pyramid For Holistic Living

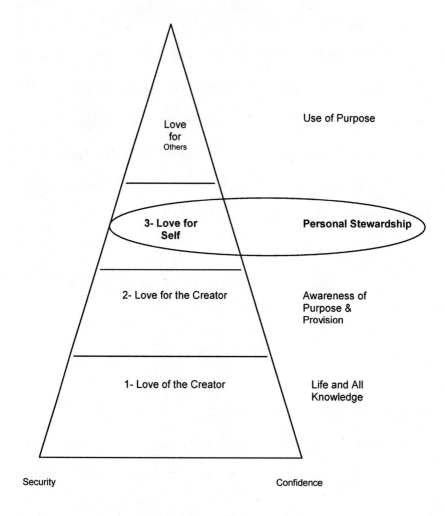

It is the *Love for Self* that allows us to be good stewards of our life and health.

Tune up Your Spirit - Identify Your Enemy

The battlefield is your body, mind and spirit. The weapon is cancer. Who is the enemy? Before you can wage war on the enemy, you must understand exactly what (or who) you are fighting. Let's explore the possibilities. There are at least two potential candidates. The enemy could be self, based on lifestyle. The other could be an attack from external forces. Most of our disease battles fall into the first category. The battle plan is different based on the enemy.

If You Are The Enemy

Self Inflicted Disease is the major cause for cancer today. Many of us, unaware, of the consequences resulting from years of abuse and neglect, ignore the body's messages. We keep going until we hit a land mine. Poor nutrition, stress, cigarettes, alcohol, sleep deprivation, un-forgiveness, self-hate, guilt and the overall devaluing of oneself contributes to a lifestyle that is primed for disease. Bad choices were made despite warnings of health hazards. Besides everyone seems to live that way!

Surina Ann Jordan

It is a tough thing to entertain thoughts of being the cause of such a dreadful disease like cancer, but awareness is half of the battle. It may seem like I am kicking you when you are down. But I am not. Remember that the truth will set you free. You were the enemy. Praying the following prayer will help us get on with your new healthy lifestyle.

Prayer of Reconciliation

Father, for some time now, I have attempted to live my life in the physical, only acknowledging you at my convenience. I have many other gods on the altar of my heart. Stress, paranoia and distrust tend to drive my thoughts and actions. I am sorry for expecting you to share your throne with these other things. I need you to cleanse me in every dimension of my being. I need you to heal every wound and disease caused by my previous ways and lack of stewardship. Then fill me with your Spirit. Teach, lead and guide me into all knowledge, wisdom and truth. Help me to apply the information you reveal to my daily living as I seek you daily in prayer and meditation. Teach me what I must do to live in health and on purpose. Thank you for my divine healing and for making me whole. In Jesus Name, Amen.

If The Attack Is From External Forces (Satan)

For many to use the word Satan is very strong and uncomfortable. And depending upon your religious orientation it may even turn you away from the rest of this book. But please be patient with me while I explain.

We all know that if your body is in pain, it is almost impossible to go about day-to-day life. It is difficult to stay focused. There is a negative force that exists in the universe. In the Christian vernacular it is referred to as Satan, the fallen angel whose mission in life is to destroy all good and beautiful things that have meaning and purpose to the Creator. You and I fit the bill. We are extremely meaningful to the Creator.

If you are doing too much good and making the positive difference in too many lives, you are a potential target for some form of attack by this force. For some it may not be an illness. It could be something that someone does to you. Something that discourages you and wounds your spirit, emotion and physical well-being (a toxic emotional relationship or work environment or a broken heart).

41

If you feel a sense of confirmation as you read this, knowing that your work is not done and your death from cancer or from anything would be untimely and premature, then don't take this diagnosis sitting down. Fight! This became evident in my husband's case.

Too much good was happening. We had just relocated to Atlanta, Georgia by my husband's new company. We had just completed a combined total of 15 years in teaching and leadership at our church in Maryland. Our daughter Roxane had just turned 5 years old. My health was improving tremendously and we had started to embrace the principles for living healthy to prevent disease. My publication work on health and nutrition fit nicely into the path set before us. It was helping many, many people. We could feel the excitement about our future and our purpose. And then he was diagnosed... Something simply did not add up!

As we sought the Creator, our strategy was made clear each day. We agreed to choose life and embrace life! We chose a piece of land, and had a home built. Our last chemo treatment was a week before settlement. We were led to a small church family who really loved us. We worked at our jobs. Took night walks on the beach, prayed, cried, laughed, ate good and rested. We were confident that the Creator was in the middle of this and that he had made an investment in us. If he was willing to fight, so were we!

Let's take the authority the Creator has given us to fulfill our divine purpose or mission and do what we need to do to heal and move on with life. Sometimes we are presented with situations that are for character building and because we are considered qualified to handle that situation. The result of the situation is a stronger person and an experience that encourages many sometimes thousands of people.

If you don't know what your divine purpose is in life; go to the Appendix 1.

Prayer Against Satan's Attack

Satan you are an enemy of God. And because I am God's child you hate me also. Everyday of my life has been planned. Before I was in the womb, it was all planned. I know that my work _____ (state it) is important and significant for this generation at this time. I know that I was chosen to perform this task and that no one has this unique task but me. In the name of Christ, I renounce and arrest your plan to destroy me and prevent me from fulfilling my divine purpose. I choose to live and not die!

Call for the elders of the church for anointing and prayer.

Now that we know the enemy, we are ready for the fight. The scriptures ask, "Are you sick? Call the church leaders together to pray and anoint you with oil in the name of the master. Believing prayer will heal you, and [the Creator] will put you on your feet (James 5:14). This does not require some special prayer cloth, ritual, personality or special imported oil from the Holy Land. All you need is a mature leader in the church who is willing to pray and to encourage you spiritually. This individual cannot heal. He or she can only call on the Creator, the Great Physician to heal you by faith. It is their obedience and faith and your obedience and faith in the Great Physician that makes it happen.

I will never forget one Saturday evening as I was preparing for church. At that time we had finally gotten the right diagnosis and I was prayerfully going through what we had done and wondering if we had omitted anything that would block my husband's healing. I realized that we had not called for the elders of the church. I did not mention this to my husband but I did say silently "OK" in my spirit (not really knowing how to make it happen). During Sunday morning church service an amazing thing happened. The Pastor came down from the pulpit with a small vial of oil, walked up to my husband, anointed his forehead and began to pray! I was stunned for a few moments. Our pastor had never done anything like this before and we have never seen him do it again. It was a confirmation to me that we were on the right track and that we had to continue on the road to his healing. If you don't have a church home, don't worry, the Creator will show you what to do to accomplish this.

Develop A Lifestyle To Support Treatment And Wellness

There is an equilibrium or normal condition of health that the body seeks to maintain. As we cooperate with normal body function an ultimate state of health and wellness is reached. Normal body function includes, proper elimination, water intake, peace, purpose, proper nourishment, sufficient sleep, relaxation and consistent exercise. These elements must be in place for a healthy immune system, which is the body's defense against invaders!

The following topics will help us put in place our strategy for healthy living:

- Eat To Live
- Get Fit To Live
- Develop Your Support Team
- Educate Yourself
- Stay Encouraged
- Make Key Decisions

Eat To Live

In **Figure 3.2** we present the **Pyramid For Healthy Eating**. The foundation to essential nutrition for all times is **Water**. Eight glasses of water distributed over the course of a day is recommended for all children 13 years old and above. Water transports oxygen and nutrients to every cell in the body and consistently helps the body eliminate waste and toxins. The body is made up of over 70% water. Harvey and Marilyn Diamond, in their book, **Fit For Life**, state that the body is over 70% water and in order to keep the body at an optimum weight and state of health, our diets must be 70% water-based foods.

Physical Activity is also essential. A lifestyle that includes exercise helps with proper digestion and elimination. It also helps to utilize calories and burns fat more efficiently, while regulating the metabolism.

Fruits and vegetables are the cornerstone of a healthy diet. They contain the cleansers and the nutrients needed for repair and proper cell replacement.

Whole Grains, Cereal & Pastas are the primary source of protein for the healthy diet.

Beans, Nuts and Seeds are good sources of carbohydrates, protein, vitamins and minerals.

The **Other Essentials** include the good fats, and various food supplements. These items help offset the nutritional shortages that are sometimes lacking in our diets (see chapter 4 for discussion on food supplementation).

You will notice the absence of any animal protein or by-products including meat, poultry, fish, eggs or dairy. The reason is because if there is cancer in the body, it is important to cut off the food source of the abnormal cells. Studies have shown that because of the additives, hormones and acid or (pH) level, animal protein is a good source of energy for cancer cells.

> *... it is important to cut off the food source of the abnormal cells.*

Refined sugar is also an excellent source of energy for cancer cells. Other sweeteners (honey, barely malt, maple syrup) may be used on a limited basis.

It is important to provide the body with the foods that help strengthen the body and provide the nutrients needed for normal cell growth.

Figure 3.2 - Pyramid for Healthy Eating

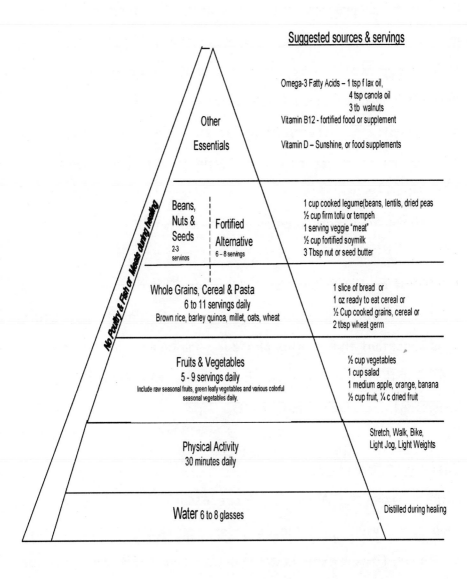

Note: Buy organic foods where possible

Surina Ann Jordan

Fit to Live

No nutritional program would be complete without an exercise program. In order to regain health and maintain it, it is important that we provide more oxygen to the blood and organs. We must detoxify the body through the sweat glands, improve circulation and regulate the appetite. Regular exercise improves digestion and elimination, increases energy levels, lowers blood cholesterol, reduces stress, anxiety and improves sleep. All this and more can be accomplished through an exercise program.

A word of caution is necessary, however. This does not mean you need to go out and join an expensive gym or hire a fitness trainer. It is important that at this phase in your healing and restoration that you do not overtax the body in any way. Low impact but consistent exercise is best.

Just Start Walking

Studies from the American Heart Association and many more recommend walking as the best form of exercise. The nation's health and fitness experts officially embraced this non-strenuous approach to exercise. Walking is best for most of us because it is already something we do.

The costs are minimal. A pair of sturdy, supportive shoes and sensible socks is all you need. The perfect shoe should fit so that your arch rests on the shoe's arch. The bottom of the shoe should be rounded to provide a smooth heel-to-toe stride. The weight of the shoe should be light. The shoes should be flexible and not stiff, which could prevent proper foot flexing. Socks should fit loosely but not be oversized.

According to a survey by the Centers for Disease Control and Prevention (CDC) in Atlanta, fewer than one-third of Americans are active enough for good health. Walking 30 minutes a day is adequate, according to the Surgeon General's Report on Physical Activity and Health. It does not have to be 30 consecutive minutes. Small lifestyle changes can help you meet this requirement easily. Here are some suggestions:

➢ Park your car a few blocks farther from your destination and walk.
➢ Walk at lunch.
➢ Become a mall walker (rain or shine).
➢ Take the stairs instead of the elevator.
➢ Walk your dog or walk around your property or Apartment complex.

Surina Ann Jordan

Other exercise ideas

Other low impact exercises include, water aerobics, tai chi (*tie chee*), light yoga, and bike riding.

Water aerobics

Water aerobics is an ideal approach to beginning an exercise program. It is ideal if you are overweight or suffer from arthritis or other skeletal problems. It allows you to exercise with less impact thus avoiding injury or damage to your joints. Water aerobics is offered at most YMCA facilities.

Tai chi (pronounced *tie chee*)

Tai chi is a calming of the mind and relaxing the body that results in the coordination of mind and body. The harmony of mind and body produces harmony of movement. At first you have to think about the movements, after a while they become instinctive and natural. The four essential points of T'ai Chi are; complete relaxation of the body; calmness of the mind; serenity of the energy; and soft and supple movement. Classes are offered in metro area communities. You can also use video recordings at home.

Yoga

The historical yoga is connected to the Hindu tradition. Yoga is typically not practiced in this country as a religion and therefore many people don't find a conflict with their religious beliefs. Today, most Yoga practices in the West focus on the physical posture, breathing exercises and meditation. Classes and/or video recordings can get you started.

Bike Riding

Bike riding can be low or high impact depending upon how aggressive you ride. It is safe and a 30 minute ride daily can be a great benefit.

Fitness Trainer

A professional fitness trainer might also be a good idea. Make sure that the trainer is certified and has references. Also make sure he or she is aware of your healing challenge and agrees to work within your limitations.

Again, regular exercise is essential to good health. It helps regulate weight, various bodily functions (digestion, elimination, detoxification) and improves sleep. It also helps boosts your immune system.

Develop Your Support Team

One thing that will become very clear as you start your new life, is that it is not business as usual. You will need a group of people that can assist and encourage you as you go. Sometimes you just need a quiet, safe shoulder so that you can exhale and cry. Or maybe just get a hug from someone who cares. Few people really understand but the Creator will send the right people along just when you need them. In Figure 3.3 we list the members of your support team. Their roles are also outlined. This team is essential during your healing and recovery period:

Figure 3.3 - Your Support Team

You	Know that the Creator is in charge, but he has made you the manager. Shut down anything that can wait until you regroup and have energy to handle it. Seek out positive people and things. Remember that to laugh or cry is therapeutic.
The Creator	Will never leave you. He is closer to you now than ever. This experience is now based on who you are to him. He has waited for this relationship all your life.
Prayer Network	It's nice that people are willing to pray for you, but for this fight, you need prayer warriors that feel led by the Creator to intercede constantly on your behalf. They understand this type of warfare and commit to do so. Get them together for meetings (in person or by phone). Develop specific prayer lists. Include each doctor's appointment, exam and test. Include wisdom and understanding, confirmations on decisions, finances, fears etc. Celebrate with praise for every little victory! At some point, the prayer focus must shift from healing to the manifestation of the healing. Let me explain. Your prayer will ask and believe the divine healer for healing. The prayer request will shift to acceptance of healing and thanksgiving. This will happen prior to the evidence of complete physical healing.
Doctors	Must be managed and appreciated for their training and practice. They have been made to feel that they are the bosses where your health is concerned. Ask questions. Explain how much you appreciate them but let them know that you see them as a partner and would like time to think over every decision and recommendation that he or she proposes. This gives you time to update

the prayer network and seek additional information and alternatives. Each visit, you will get certain information about your vitals, like blood pressure, blood count, temperature and weight, which helps indicate the condition of the immune system and other test results.

DO NOT stay away from your doctor. If you are not comfortable, get another one, but do not go this alone. Manage the alternative caregivers also. All alternative practitioners attempt to strengthen the immune system so that your body can heal itself. Determine which is best for you.

FAMILY AND HELPERS

Let people help. These are people that will help you do the things you would normally do for yourself. Their sole purpose is to reduce your stress and encourage. If you are single, it can be a greater adjustment. For years you may have made yourself extremely independent of others. Some days, you may become totally reliant on others. They are like angels from the Lord. They are not necessarily good on advice and may or may not be in your prayer network. From cooking to driving they are there for you. They also help encourage you as you struggle to hold on to some of the normal routines. Always take someone with you to your doctor's appointments, exams and consultations. They can hear and possibly ask questions that you may not think of or remember and help maintain a log of events.

Educate Yourself

- Log - keep a journal or log book of all that you experience. Note your appointments, test results and how you are feeling (i.e. night sweats, fevers, medicine and remedies used).

- Resources - the health food store book rooms for alternatives and the public library are good sources of information.

- Internet - search for information on support groups and the latest publications, research, medical information and alternative treatments relating to your diagnosis.

- National Institute of Health - primarily information and many publications related to traditional medicine.

Stay Encouraged

- You are a fighter. Some days you will have to take one minute at a time. Any more than that would be overwhelming.

- Seek wise counsel and then make your decisions.

- Stay Encouraged and learn to laugh several times each day.

- Stay close to the Creator. Rest in his peace and your purpose. No matter what the situation, hold to the love he has provided.

We all know someone who we truly believe found healing in death. These people were promoted to the kingdom of heaven. They were able to shed the physical completely and free the spirit. Praise God, it is all good, "for to be absent from the physical is to be present with the Lord (II Corinthians 5:8).

Develop A Personal Prayer Life and Relationship with God

You cannot do this without a higher power. You want to be made whole, which is not possible without the power of God. You may achieve a state of remission however, wholeness requires healing of the body, soul and spirit. Separation from God produces fear and anxiety. It also increases the chance for sickness and disease.

The following scriptures are promises and meditations that the Creator made to us who wish to abide in his love:

Beloved, I wish above all things that thou mayest prosper and be in health, even as thy soul prospereth (3 John 1:2).

Surina Ann Jordan

Fear thou not; for I am with thee: be not dismayed; for I am thy God: I will strengthen thee; yea I will help thee; yea, I will uphold thee with the right hand of my righteousness. (Isaiah 41:10).

"But I will restore you to health and heal your wounds," declares the Lord. (Jeremiah 30:17).

Your word is a lamp to my feet and a light to my path (Psalms 119:105).

Suggested Prayer:

Great Divine Healer, I know that you know what you are doing with me. You know that I want to be healed and made whole. Help me to rest in you and receive it.

Make Key Decisions – A Matter of Stewardship

As discussed in previous chapters, love is the fuel we need to fight on. Personal stewardship is necessary in order to experience healing and restoration to where the Creator had intended for you to be. There are several stewardship issues that should be discussed, which require decisions. Failure to decide is a decision not to decide, which puts the decision in the hands of someone else and causes confusion that could be avoided.

Quality of Life

At some point all the options and information before you boils down to a few basic decision points. One of the key decisions is: Based on where I find myself today (state of health, age, opportunity), how do I want to live the rest of my life?

Some of the side effects of treatments can be more traumatic then your cancer diagnosis. Many people die from the treatment. On the other hand, many people die *with* cancer not from cancer. A side effect of chemotherapy could be cancer.

Surina Ann Jordan

Living Will

A living will is a document written by you that states your preferences as to how you would like to be treated and to what extent if for some reason you are in a position where you cannot communicate your wishes. For example many people have been connected to life support systems for years based on the fact that they never indicated what should be done if they could not communicate. To know your preferences makes it much easier on the family. A living will simply states that you would not like to be resuscitated or that you would like to be resuscitated. Your signature and a date are required. Some states may require a notary and/or witnesses.

Last Will and Testament

Sick or not, it is your responsibility to make sure that the testimony/health witness is laced within the process. I am not recommending this because of your diagnosis. Drawing up a last will and testament is a matter of stewardship. Sick or well all adults should do this and keep it current. When I realized I had some say in how my final arrangements would be made, I began to reflect on the most disturbing part of funerals (or home-going) services I had ever attended. As an officer in the church for

62

more than 10 years, I have attended a lot of them. For example, I personally do not want to be viewed after my death. I feel that this gets out of hand today. I have seen some coffins reopened after the eulogy for a final good bye! It tears your loved ones heart out, all over again. So I have specifically stated that this is not to be done. I have also stated my menu preferences for the after meal, so that the witness of my life is continued. Good stewardship in this area removes the burden and stress and takes away the guesswork from those you care about.

Chapter 3 - Summary Next Steps - Principles for Living

Love is the Foundation For Holistic Living • Love of the Creator • Love for the Creator • Love for Self • Love for Others
Enemies that cause sickness and disease: • The Enemy Within (you could be the enemy) • External Negative Forces
The Lifestyle That Supports Treatment and Wellness: • Peace of Mind • Spiritual Support of the Elders or Spiritual Leaders • Protecting Your Feelings • Modifying Your Lifestyle (Eat/Fit) • Form Your Support Team • Educating Yourself • Stay Encouraged
Good stewardship includes making the following decisions: • Determine Your Quality of Life • Determine and Document Your Living Will • Determine and Document Your Last Will and Testament

Chapter 4

Most Frequently Asked Questions

Chapter 4

Most Frequently Asked Questions

Where do I get food that is produced without chemicals (organic food)?

Many natural food products are appearing on the shelves of major grocery stores and department stores like Wal-Mart and Target. This is encouraging news; however there are many products that cannot be found anywhere except the natural food or health food store.

A natural food store provides food products that are less processed than foods at traditional grocery stores. These foods contain few preservatives and are often organically grown and manufactured with nutrition as priority. Produce is more fresh and mostly pesticide free. The store presents choice without a strong marketing influence. Depending on the size, these stores may also contain natural pharmacies for herbs, various remedies, tinctures and bulk food items.

As we embrace healthier lifestyles it is important that we become comfortable and knowledgeable about these products and where to get them. We need to visit the natural foods store periodically for certain staples. Be selective, read the labels. Reading labels in a store like this can be a real education. You will notice that unlike the traditional grocery store, you can recognize and pronounce every ingredient. Keep in mind however, that there is no legal definition for the word "natural" (even with the Food and Drug Administration). This term can mean anything that the manufacturer wants it to mean. However, there is a standard for organic. Anything labeled organic must adhere to these codes and farmers must become certified as a producer and manufacturer of organic goods.

Farmer's Market
Health Food or Natural Food Stores
Websites - www.shopnatural.com

Must a person healing from cancer eat all raw foods?

No, however the primary source of fuel for the body should be made up of raw fruits, vegetables and sprouted grains and nuts. Here is why.

Cooking at temperatures higher than 112 degrees destroys all food enzymes.

Vitamins and minerals remain in cooked food but the food enzymes do not. The pancreas has to manufacture a customized set of digestive enzymes to digest a cooked meal. As a result the metabolic enzymes needed for building and repair are often times not available. The pancreas, which spends most of its time preparing enzymes for digestion, gets overworked. It becomes enlarged and taxes every organ in the body to deal with our poor food choices. The body is preoccupied with digesting food. Not enough energy is left to guard the body. Our poor diets make us susceptible to disease. Foreign invaders cause organs to malfunction. And sickness and disease are allowed to exist in the body.

By eating more raw foods the body can continue to heal and guard us against illness and degenerative diseases. The following is a list of foods you can include with your meals. Bananas, avocados, grapes, pineapple, mangoes, uncooked dark leafy vegetables, cabbage, carrots, fresh fruit or vegetable juices. Also include fresh raw dates, fresh raw figs, raw honey, raw nut butter, soaked raw cereal grains, seeds and nuts. These items can be eaten alone or as a part of a cooked enzyme-less meal.

Another source of enzyme-rich food are fresh fruit and vegetable juices. Many nutrients are lost within 15 minutes of juicing which is why juicing at the point of consumption is key. Use fruit juice for cleansing and vegetable juice for healing and restoration.

Lightly steamed vegetables and cooked organic whole grains, like brown rice and cous cous are good choices. Note that whenever cooked food is eaten, a digestive enzyme supplement should be used. Supplementing with digestive enzymes allows the body to spend its energy healing rather than digesting food.

What if I have no appetite?

Even though you may not have an appetite or feel like eating, the body needs fuel to build healthy cells and to maintain your energy levels, therefore some food must be eaten several times each day. At this point your appetite must not control your diet. You must eat for energy and healing. You need good chemical-free food everyday.

Surina Ann Jordan

Are food combinations important?

During your healing, quality food must be eaten in order so that proper digestion can take place. This will also help maintain the energy level for healing and repair. For example, never eat fruit with other foods. The reason is the fruit is the perfect food for the body and needs no assistance to assimilate digestion. If you mix it with foods then the fruit is held up and remains in the digestive tract and becomes rotten or putrefies, which no longer has nutritional value. So eat fruit on empty stomach or at least 3 hours after any other meal. In the morning the body is in an elimination mode. Fruit requires little attention and does not slow down the elimination process but rather helps out by adding more water and roughage. Eat a variety and as much as you want. By lunch time, the body is ready to receive a heavy meal. Include a fresh salad or vegetable juice at the beginning of the meal. Figure 4.1 list the types of food that could be eaten for each meal.

Figure 4.1 Best Food for Each Meal

Steps	Breakfast	Lunch	Dinner	Snacks
1	Fruit and/ fresh fruit juice and/or smoothie	Raw/and or Fresh Vegetable Juice	Raw/and or Fresh Vegetable Juice	Juice or fruit
2*	Light grain	Cooked Food	Cooked Food	Grains, nuts and/or raisins
3	Drink	Drink	Drink	Drink

There are some combinations of foods that lead to successful digestion and others that do not. Figure 4.2 list the proper food combinations that move the food along and provide proper absorption of nutrients for the body.

*Food Supplements are taken at the beginning of step 2.

Figure 4.2 – Food Combining Chart

√	Fruit	+	Fruit
X	Fruit	+	Vegetable
X	Fruit	+	Protein
X	Fruit	+	Starch
√	Vegetable	+	Protein
√	Vegetable	+	Starch
√	Vegetable	+	Vegetable
X	Protein	+	Starch
X	Protein	+	Protein

During your restoration period, an enzyme supplement is recommended whenever you eat cooked food. Dinner is a repeat of lunch, but should be less. Also eat dinner before 7 p.m. if possible. This gives your body ample time to complete the digestive process before bedtime.

Never drink when eating. It neutralizes the digestive fluids that the body produces to efficiently digest your food.

What about carbohydrates?

All carbohydrates are not created equal. The best sources for carbohydrates are legumes (beans), whole grains, vegetables, fruits, nuts and seeds.

Avoid those products that have been refined resulting in starches and sugars with no fiber. More than 70% of the nutrients are lost during the refinement process. When these products (examples: white flour, white sugar, white bread and white rice) are used to make various foods, they become health hazards.

Should I supplement my diet with food supplements?

There are many schools of thought on whether a person should take vitamins and other food supplements. You must decide for yourself, however I am of the opinion that it is a good idea to supplement your diet. The average American diet lacks many key combinations of nutrients that are required to build and maintain healthy cells. A multi-vitamin and green food (chlorophyll) supplement is needed.

A good source of chlorophyll and a multi-vitamin would be the basics. The purpose of a chlorophyll supplement is to make up for the lack of green vegetables we need but don't get. Chlorophyll is the blood of the plant. Hemoglobin is the blood of humans. Chemically, their make up is almost identical; therefore it is one of the most perfect food sources. There are many types at the health food store like, green barley, wheat grass and spirulina. As you begin to add more dark leafy greens and broccoli to your diet; you can reduce the amount of chlorophyll supplements.

Where can I find some recipes that are healthy with less animal protein that taste good?

The following websites are full of recipes using fresh vegetables, fruits and grains.

Vegetarian food websites that may be of interest to you:

vegweb.com   veganoutreach.com   vegefood.com

vrg.org   veganmania.com

veg-it.com   vegFamily.com

Terms you should know:

Vegan – one who does not eat meat, seafood, poultry or by-products (dairy, eggs) of animals. They eat vegetables, fruits and grains. This is the safest way to eat during your healing period.

Vegetarian – one who does not eat meat, seafood or poultry, but does eat animal by-products.

Lacto – means dairy

Ovo - means eggs

Depending on the circle of people, the definition of vegetarian will fluctuate. Some include seafood or poultry. Some may be lacto-vegetarians, which means they do not consume milk, cheese or other dairy products.

Will I ever be able to eat meat again?

This is your decision to make. Hopefully you will discover a whole world of food choices. Know that the creator can help you change your appetite for meat.

There are some meats that are produced without chemicals. There are some seafoods that are safer than others, for example fish with fins instead of shellfish that eat from the ocean floor or fish from lakes, which tend to be more polluted than ocean water.

If after your healing you decide to include some meat, it must be occasional and in small portions. Take a look at the diet of people from the orient. They are some of the healthiest people in the world. When meat or fish is consumed, it is in pieces. They can use one chicken breast to feed 10 or more people! Grains and vegetables make up the majority of the meal. This type of eating is less taxing on the body. Large portions of animal protein take a great deal of energy from the body to digest and discard.

Should I fire my medical doctor?

It is not recommended that you completely sever your relationship with your doctor. Partnering with a medical doctor can increase your knowledge and resources for your healing process. See her as a partner on your healing team.

How should I relate to my medical doctor?

Keeping the peace is very important. Try not to make your medical doctor angry. However, keep these things in mind as you build your relationship with your doctor. Doctors are often "the enemy" unaware. Their goal is to extend life vs. quality of life so they will not think to explain to you all the consequences and or impacts of certain treatments. They are human. However, from medical school to every other patient they have been given the impossible god-like responsibility of healing people. The tools they have include studies from other cases and research, pharmaceuticals, computer technology for the diagnosis of symptoms and surgery.

Therefore, depending on the age and years of practice, your doctor will not be accustomed to patients who are informed and knowledgeable about their situation. So listen intently and ask questions. Know that at the end of the day, you make the final decision and if your ability to decide is what makes them angry, then so be it. If you feel a good relationship of mutual respect is not possible, find another doctor.

Also see questions for doctor's visits at the end of chapter 1.

If I elect chemotherapy and/or radiation what are the typical side effects?

The short-term possible side effects include, mouth sores, gastritis, fevers & infections, constipation, nausea, digestive problems, headaches, joint pain and depression. Also included are hair loss, dark/collapsed veins, discolored fingernails and toenails and numbness in the fingers and toes. These side effects typically go away once the treatments are discontinued.

The long-term side effects are many and have not all been attributed to chemotherapy. However **the major long-term side effect is cancer and liver damage.**

What natural remedies could I use to help with the side effects?

Chemo Side Effect	Remedy	Comments
Mouth Sores, Gastritis,	Acidophilus	Friendly bacteria is needed in the intestines. Acidophilus restores the good bacteria back into the colon and helps fight food poisoning or other side effects like yeast infections from antibiotics. Take daily as a preventive measure.
Fever and infections	Peppermint Tea, Garlic & Echinacea/ Goldenseal supplements	Helps cleanse the body of infections and boost the immune system. Short term use (3 weeks) is best.
Constipation	Herbal or Vegetable Stool Softener /Laxative	Use an herbal or vegetable laxative or stool softener prior to each chemotherapy treatment and after treatment in order to maintain bowel functions. See questions on food combining.
Mal nutrition	Green Barley	In order to rebuild the body, the proper nutrients from a variety of fruits, & vegetables is essential. If your doctor says "no raw vegetables or fruit"- green barley is the perfect supplement. It is organic, high in chlorophyll and is made from the juice of young organic barley plants.
	Spirulina	Organic sea weed loaded with all the minerals and B vitamins. Pill or powder.
Nausea; digestive problems; Adrenal & Liver Support	Nux Vomica,	Nausea is not a stomach problem from chemo, but rather a symptom of toxicity in the body and an overworked liver. Nux Vomica is a homeopathic remedy with no side

		effects that eliminates nausea. Strength=30c
	Ginger	Ginger is also good for nausea and digestion. Slice ½ " thick piece of ginger about the size of a quarter add to hot water and sweetener (raw honey) to taste.
Headaches	Water	Increase water intake.
Joint pain	Arnica Montana	Homeopathic remedy with no side affects that removes pains and aches. Strength=30c
Depression	Moderate sunshine, walk or exercise and laughter.	Volunteer at a homeless shelter or reform school or orphanage. Spend time with positive family and friends. (see support team discussion)
	St John's Wort	See your alternative practitioner for the right dosage for you.

There are some side effects however, for which I have not found a remedy. These include hair loss, dark/collapsed veins, discolored fingernails and toenails and numbness in the fingers and toes.

The conventional approach to dealing with the side effects of chemotherapy is primarily through the use of pharmaceuticals. Know that there are side effects to these pharmaceuticals and that they have the potential to further weaken the body's ability to fight the disease.

What alternative treatments and remedies does my health insurance company cover?

In general, not many are covered. Health insurance has originated from conventional medicine. It is set up for underwriting medical treatments and not prevention. Understand your insurance coverage. For example what is covered and what is not covered if you don't accept full treatment, second opinions and/or alternatives.

In anticipation of extra expenses, you should budget for alternatives treatments or supplements.

Progress is being made. Ten years ago chiropractic treatment, which is considered an alternative treatment, is now covered under most medical insurances. There are some companies that cover alternative medicine if the doctor will assist you with filing the claims.

What are the stages of cancer?

Stage I the malignancy is considered isolated and is treatable.

Stage II the tumors are into the muscle wall.

Stage III involves the lymph nodes.

Stage IV is advanced cancer. The cancer has metastasized and has typically spread to major organs including the liver. Conventional treatment at this stage is for life extension and mostly experimental.

For more information about staging for a specific cancer diagnosis, go to http://www.nci.nih.gov/dictionary/, select S and page down to the word staging.

What if I have been diagnosed with "stage 4" cancer?

Doctors and hospitals will use every tool available to them to extend your life, but even they will admit that their treatment is buying you a little more time not a cure. Your choice and the reality is that you are going to die if you go totally the traditional medicine route. The treatment will more than likely weaken your ability to fight the cancer and give the body less of an opportunity to heal itself.

With that as a backdrop, there are some alternatives. There are countless testimonies of people who have simply walked away from the chemo and other poisons, purchased a juicer and started one day at a time juicing organic dark green vegetables, carrots and fruit several times each day and eating mostly raw foods, no processed foods, refined sugar or animal protein of any kind. This regiment typically starves the cancer cells and begins to arrest them. With an increase in consumption of pure water, more rest, relaxation, a positive attitude and lots of prayer, five, ten years later they are still juicing and living life to its fullest.

There are several **alternatives**, however the most successful combination that I have observed is this:

-Get a juicer and **juice** carrot, dark greens (spinach, kale, collards ...) add an apple or a little honey for taste; also juice fresh oranges. Drink as much as you can everyday.

-Take **barley green powder** or pills (barley life). This can be taken with water or the fresh juices. This is chemically like putting fresh blood in the system. It will help build healthy cells and restore energy levels.

-Take **God's blessing tea**. A strong antioxidant created by a man (minister) in Florida that is helping people who were considered terminal purge themselves of tumors and other diseases.

-Take high dosages of **Vitamin C powder** (as much as the bowels can stand). And drink plenty of pure water.

-**Exercise**. Walking will do. Just do it everyday if possible for at least 30 minutes in fresh air.

-**Sleep more**. At least 8 to 10 hours a day if possible.

-**Reduce Stress**. Many of us live with more stress than the body can handle.

During my husband's healing, we used them all.

What is meant by environmentally friendly?

Those things that cause no harm to life around them are considered environmentally friendly. Many products and foods contain highly toxic chemicals. Many are avoidable if we are aware of their existence. Read the labels of all foods and products that you use.

There is a level of toxic exposure that must be kept at a minimum if we are going to remain disease free and feeling good about life.

Because there are so many harmful **exposures that we cannot control**, we must put in place a plan to avoid or limit **those things we can control.**

During your healing don't expose yourself to unnecessary toxins by painting the house or replacing the carpeting, doing your nails or dying hair. Do not smoke or drink. If you do, the body has to put fighting cancer on hold to address the new threats.

At the natural grocery, you can find chemical-free toiletries without perfumes and household cleansers that are environment friendly.

How do I start living?

Go to Chapter 3 and start there.

What type of lifestyle should I have now?

You should consider the principles for healthy living in chapter 3.

If I choose alternative treatments, how do I monitor progress towards health?

Regardless of what path you take to treatment, it is important to maintain a relationship with your medical doctor. You will want to be tested periodically for progress and to get the state of things based on diagnostic tests.

Naturopathic doctors will also have specific ways to measure your progress.

Figure 4.3 Questions for Follow-up Visits contains a list of questions that will help you record information about your vital signs and other items that help determine your state of health.

Figure 4.3 - Questions for Follow-up Visits

1. What are my vital statistics?

White Cell Count:	Red Cell Count:
Temperature:	Blood Pressure:
Weight:	PSA Levels:

2. Opinion of Progress?

Stage ___? Any metastasis? (spreading to other organs or parts of the body)?

3. Opinion of Progress Relative to Other Cases?

4. Recommended Next Steps?

5. Next Visit?

6. Purpose of Next Visit?

7. What decisions need to be made?

8. What are my options?

Notes:

_____

_____

_____

_____

_____

Conclusion

A Lifestyle To Celebrate

Conclusion – A Lifestyle To Celebrate

It is not the one thing we do that threatens our health. It is not one food item that we eat or the lack of fresh fruits and vegetables. Nor is it one product that we use. It's not the chemicals that we are exposed to; be it hair perms, insecticides, ammonia, or air fresheners. It is not the amount of substances or medications that we take. Nor is it the lack of water or the amount of coffee we drink. It's not the air pollution from cars & trucks, hazardous wastes, ultraviolet radiation or landfills. It is not the lack of sleep, rest or quiet time. It is not too much stress or work, nor is it the lack of exercise.

It is the collective use and exposure to all these things that puts the body at risk and encourages abnormal cell growth. It is the careless treatment of our spirit, mind and body that breaks down the immune system. This leaves little time for healing, repair and the replacement of healthy cells. And when the body does attempt to rebuild there is little fuel from whole foods and no reserves to complete the task.

The immune system is not being supported and therefore cannot function at its full capacity in order to fight off many of the threats to the body. The loss of good health is so gradual that it can go unnoticed. A sense of what feels normal is lost and often times the onset of a particular symptom cannot be pinpointed.

Many of the items listed above strip the body of key nutrients and minerals that are needed in order to maintain good health.

> *It is the combined result of the day-to-day exposure, tearing down and not repairing, that makes us vulnerable to disease.*

At this point we must start living. The length of our lives is not as important as we often think. Length of life is not equal to quality of life. Really living is embracing the principles for living, which includes an awareness of purpose and making choices about daily living. Many of the things that we are exposed to can be avoided or replaced by more natural alternatives. This takes knowledge and understanding, which allows us to live a physical existence, entrenched in love and good stewardship.

With the Creator as your coach to bring forth the peace, purpose and plan for your life ...

Congratulations! Now you can start living.

Resources for Research and Treatment

Books

Name	Author	Description
Alternative Books		
Alternatives in Cancer Therapy	Ross Pelton & Lee Overholser	Provides information on the research, efficacy, potential side effects, and availability of each treatment
Options	Richard Walters	Alternative Cancer Therapies
Living Foods Lifestyle	Brenda Cobb	An inspiring guide filled with remarkable stories and delicious raw and living food recipes
Bragg Healthy Lifestyle	Paul & Patricia Bragg	Body purification, toxic less diet & healing system
Conventional Books		
Cancer: The Facts	Michael Whitehouse & Maurice Slevin,	Oxford University Press, 1996

| Cancer: What Every Patient Needs to Know (Rev edn) | Jeffrey Tobias | Bloomsbury, 1999 |

Inspirational Books

God's Psychiatry	Charles Allen	"Dr. Allen's advice is as warm as it is practical. Each page is a challenge – and an inspiration."
The Seeds for Your Potential	Myles Monroe	A book that helps you identify your divine purpose or passion in life.
Prayers That Avail Much	Word Ministries Harrison House	Prayers using bible verses. Prayers for life's situations.

General Internet Research

Use a web search engine, key in your diagnosis. For example, breast cancer or prostate cancer. Some popular search engines include:

www.yahoo.com   www.dogpile.com
www.google.com

Websites - Conventional Medicine

www.cancerbacup.org.uk
CancerBACUP
Contains over 2000 pages of accurate, up to date information on all aspects of cancer.

www.crc.org
Cancer Research Campaign
Has news about recent research, types of cancer, treatments and prevention of cancer.

www.mayo.edu
Mayo Clinic
Mayo Cancer Center is an international leader in cancer treatment and research.

www.intelihealth.com
InteliHealth
Drug and medical information. Easy to use

and free from medical jargon. Have patient information leaflets, which can be printed.

www.nci.nih.gov
National Cancer Institute - National Institute of Health (USA).
Gives comprehensive information on cancer and treatment. Good information to help you understand how your medical doctor approaches care

www.webmd.com
Pharmaceuticals and Prescription Drugs
A dictionary/informational site to look up prescriptions. Provides side effects, drug interactions and various warnings.

Websites, Centers and Resources – Alternative Medicine

Name	Contact Information	Description/Comments
Dr. Nicholas Gonzalez Life Extension Practitioner	(212) 213-3337 www.dr-gonzalez.com	"Dr. Gonzalez's therapy is built around the concept of making the body eradicate its own illness, rather than obliterating it with outside forces. His therapy has gotten the attention of the National Cancer Institute. Diet is one of his primary weapons. Research demonstrates that selected foods (along with other factors) can actually turn the tide against cancer. Food can create such an inoperable environment for cancer that it gives up. This is partly due to the fact that food changes the biochemistry of the entire body not just one part. This insures that the cancer cannot simply move to another area of the body."

Surina Ann Jordan

Websites, Centers and Resources – Alternative Medicine

Rev George H. Malkmus Hallelujah Acres Health Ministry	(704) 481-1700; www.hacres.com	"Diagnosed with colon cancer over 20 years ago. After watching his mother die and suffer so terribly from medical treatment of cancer he was determined not to go that way. He searched for and found an alternative. Today he has written several books and trains thousands of people every year on nutrition and changing lifestyle God's way." Author of **Why Christians Get Sick**.

| Dr. Sebi The Fig Tree and Usha Herbal Research Institute | USHA / The Figtree (800) 515-SEBI or 310-838-2490 www.drsebi.com | "Dr. Sebi came to the United States as a 20 year old self -educated man who was diagnosed with asthma, diabetes, impotency and obesity. After unsuccessful treatments with conventional doctors, Sebi was lead to a herbologist in Mexico. Finding great healing success from all of his ailments, he began creating a natural herbal compound from electric foods geared for intra-cellular cleansing and the revitalization of all the cells that make up the human body. Sebi has successfully treated thousands of people in the US and around the world for pathologies such as Aids, Cancer, Diabetes, Leukemia, Sickle Cell Anemia and many other types of illnesses like female and male dysfunctions etc." |

Websites, Centers and Resources – Alternative Medicine

| Dr. Lorraine Day, M.D | 800-574-2437 www.drday.com testimonial www.healthwisdom.com | "Dr. Day was diagnosed with invasive breast cancer but rejected standard therapies because of their destructive side effects." She is the author of the video entitled, **Why Cancer Doesn't Scare Me Anymore.** |

| Vivian Conner M.ED. Lifestyle Educator & Research Coordinator | (770) 413-6192 Georgia cfpsi@aol.com | Atlanta, email: | After her lifetime mission as a classroom teacher was cut short due to the effects of three chronic diseases (sickle cell anemia, arthritis, and breast cancer) she was led to search for better health. Through common sense, detailed reading and research, she learned and practiced the principles for a healthy living and began to rebuild her health. Her **new** mission is to help others by providing them with quality information so that they may then use it to make informed decisions concerning their own health. Vivian studied with the USHA Herbal Research Institute, is currently studying at the Trinity School of Natural Health and is a member of the Eat To Live Network. |

Ruscombe Mansion Community Health Center	4801 and 4803 Yellowwood Ave, Baltimore, MD 21209 410-367-7300	"An integrative approach to health care is provided by licensed holistic professional."
Oasis Contreras Clinic, Tijuana, Mexico	(800) 700 -1850 www.cancure.org/ oasis_hospital.htm	"Is one of the most recognized pioneers of alternative medicine in this century. According to medical charts at Oasis, Dr. Contreras Sr. Has treated more than 80,000 American patients since 1963. The Contreras therapy treats the whole patient. This is only possible when physicians utilize a special combination of science, medicine, nutrition, faith and compassion. The Contreras total care approach is based on two fundamental principles: Do no harm to your patients (Hippocrates) Love your patients as yourself (Jesus) Patients experience a therapy that is uplifting not only to the immune system but also to the spirit."
The Harold Manner Memorial Hospital	Located in Tijuana Mexico Phone:011-526-680-4422 Mailing Address: Manner Clinic P.O. box 434290 San Ysidro, California 92143	"This is an inpatient facility. The clinic specializes in malignant and nonmalignant degenerative diseases using nontoxic therapies."

Dr. Max Gerson. The Gerson Therapy	1-888-4-GERSON www.gerson.org 1572 Second Avenue, San Diego, CA 92101	"Dr. Max Gerson was first published on the topic of cancer in 1945, almost forty years before the adoption of the current official U.S. National Cancer Institute program on diet, nutrition, and cancer. Max Gerson said, "Stay close to nature and its eternal laws will protect you." He considered that degenerative diseases were brought on by toxic, degraded food, water, and air. The Gerson Therapy seeks to regenerate the body to health, supporting each important metabolic requirements by flooding the body with nutrients from almost 20 pounds of organically grown fruits and vegetables daily. Most are used to make fresh raw juice, one glass every hour, 13 times per day. He learned that the diet not only eliminated his own migraine headaches, but most other physical problems as well, including diabetes, arthritis and even terminal cancers. **The results they are getting even with terminal illnesses are spectacular.**"

Optimum Health Institute of Austin	OHI SAN DIEGO 6970 Central Avenue, Lemon Grove CA 91945 Phone (619) 464-3346 Fax (619) 589-4098 OHI AUSTIN 265 Cedar Lane Cedar Creek, TX 78612 Phone (512) 303-4817 Fax (512) 303-1239 www.optimumhealth.org	"Hippo crates, know as the "Father of Medicine", taught that wholesome natural foods could restore vibrant health. Experience with a live-food program - eliminating meat, dairy products and all processed and cooked foods has confirmed for us and tens of thousands of others that good health is a natural state. The human body is self-regenerating and self-cleansing. If given the proper tools with which to work, it can maintain its natural state of well being."
Hippocrates Health Institute	1443 Palmdale Court West Palm Beach, FL 33411 phone: 800-842-2125 or 561-471-8876 fax - 561-471-9464 www.hippocratesinst.com	"Here at Hippocrates you are introduced to a program designed to attain and maintain optimum health. The three week program will jump start your life -long journey of sensible, sane and humane living habits that will bring joy and health back into your life. They treat cancer, heart disease, diabetes, obesity, allergies, and more. We are not sure if the facilities are set up for advanced cancer."

Surina Ann Jordan

Ann Wigmore Natural Health Institute, Inc.	PO Box 429 Rincón, Puerto Rico 00677 (787) 868-6307 **www.annwigmore.org**	"Ann Wigmore is the founder of the Living Foods Lifestyle. Her 35 years of research indicate that all disease is a result of toxicity and deficiency, due to cooked and processed foods, drugs and negative mental attitudes. When her body was healed of cancer, arthritis, migraine headaches, hypoglycemia, allergies, and other conditions by way of consuming raw and living foods, she discovered that **diseases were nothing but the body's starvation of the necessary nutrients, due to lack of nourishment.** High enzyme, chlorophyll rich, easy to digest nourishment is the cornerstone of this program. Through this simple, natural lifestyle, thousands of people around the world have taken control of their lives and health."

Wildwood Lifestyle Center and Hospital	P.O. Box 129 Wildwood, GA 30757 (800) 634-9355. www.wildwoodlsc.org	"A Christian nonprofit state licensed facility dedicated to preventive medicine, natural remedies, education and Jesus Christ. This 10 to 17 day live in program emphasizes permanent lifestyle changes for achieving and maintaining good health and weight loss, using low-fat, cholesterol free, vegetarian foods, as well as instruction in nutrition, stress management, cooking, and exercise. The program includes medical evaluation and laboratory tests."

Surina Ann Jordan

Health Quarters Ministries Lodge Anne Frahm	(719) 593-8694 Colorado Springs, Co www.healthquarters.org/lodge.htm	"A 10 day residential program at the HQM Lodge in Colorado, Springs. In which participants learn and begin to put into practice specific diet and lifestyle changes aimed at helping them win back their health. When Anne Frahm discovered she had cancer, it had already gnawed from her breasts into nearly every area of her upper body. Doctors prescribed the traditional treatments of surgery, chemotherapy, and radiation, but Anne's health only worsened. Yet throughout the course of her disease, she persisted in researching a connection between cancer and nutrition. She formulated a comprehensive battle plan, and within five weeks of implementing it, her cancer disappeared without a trace. Anne and David Frahm are founders and directors of Health Quarters Ministries. Author of **The Cancer Battle Plan.**"

Information and Remedies Only		
Donna Green Goodman Lifestyle Principles, Inc	4296-B Memorial Drive Decatur, GA 30032 (404) 299-0188 email: lifeprin@aol.com	"Completely cured of breast cancer through faith, nutrition and lifestyle changes. A lifestyle for Better Health Center that offers rehab, health education and physician services. We teach simple, practical, medically proven lifestyle habits that can prevent or reverse chronic diseases. It is our belief that through a combination of lifestyle habits, simple remedies and faith, optimal health is possible." Author of: **Something To Shout About.**
God's Herbal Blessing Tea Rev. Jones	The Old Path 55 Brent Lane Pensacola, Florida, USA 32503 (850) 457-1515 Email: oldpath2002@yahoo.com Website: www.oldpath.com	"Rev. Jones was inspired by God over 15 years ago with the formula for a tea that even doctors couldn't explain why people are being healed. So many people have been cured. He was recently featured on the TV news for this restorative/miracle tea. Can be shipped anywhere."

AIM - Barley Green	Distributor: ETLNS (410) 254-2306 counselor@eattolive network.com	Whole foods supplement, rich in enzymes. Captures the nutrient barley green is a whole food concentrate; that is, it in as close to its natural state as possible and thus supplies the nutrients in natural proportions. This is an intricate part of the "hallelujah diet".
Queen Afua	106 Kingston Ave Brookland, NY 11213	"Queen Afua is a nationally renowned herbalist, holistic health specialist, and dedicated healer of women's bodies and souls, who practices from a uniquely Afro centric spiritual perspective."
American Holistic Health Association	www.ahha.org	"A nonprofit association established to promote holistic living through information sharing. Great online library of information."
The Cancer Cure Foundation	www.cancure.org contact (800) 282-2873 email at ccf@cancure.org.	"The ultimate one-stop source for information about alternative cancer treatments, therapies and clinics."
Seventh Generation	www.seventhgen.com	"Environmentally-friendly information for a safer household."

Glossary of Terms

Name	Description
Acupuncture	An alternative treatment that inserts tiny hair-like needles into various areas of the body that stimulate the body's immune system in order to restore good health. Chinese practitioners use acupuncture to treat a wide range of illnesses.
Alternative Therapy	Usually includes all non-conventional treatments i.e. enzymes, diet (and supplements), detoxification, change in life style, stress control, prevention, and biofeedback.
Animal Protein	Meat from animals, beef, poultry, pork, and seafood.
Antioxidant	The nutrients the body uses to cleanse the blood of poisons and toxins that have ended up in our bodies from food, water and the environment. They protect our health by arresting the production of potential abnormal cells

called free radicals.

Auto graft	See Autologous transplant
Autologous transplant	A procedure in which bone marrow is removed from a person, stored, and then given back to the person after intensive treatment.
Bio-magnet therapy	Treatment that applies micro-frequencies used to destroy abnormal cells and harmful organisms.
Bone marrow	The soft, sponge-like tissue in the center of most large bones. It produces white blood cells, red blood cells, and platelets.
Chemotherapy/chemo	The use of highly toxic chemicals to destroy abnormal cells.
Clinical Nutrition	A combination of processes by which the body receives and uses the substances necessary for its function, for energy, and for growth and repair of the body.
Cous cous	A rice-like grain that is flavorful and rich in nutrients. Originated from Morocco, Spain region.

Detoxification Process	Internal cleansing of body organs and systems by using various combinations including food, herbs, and hydrotherapy.
Digestive enzyme	Supplement that helps the body digest protein, carbohydrates and gats requiring less of the body's energy to do so.
External-beam radiation therapy	Radiation therapy that uses a machine to aim high-energy rays at the cancer. Also called external radiation.
Herb/herbal	Plants used for food, prescription & remedies.
Homeopathy	A natural treatment that stimulates the body's healing power.
Hormone	A chemical substance produced by the body that regulates the activities of an organ or a group of cells.
Hydrotherapy	Normally refers to the process of cleaning the colon using water. Unlike an enema which cleanses the lower colon and the rectum, a colonic cleanse all 5 ft of the colon.

Immune system

enhancement

Light therapy	Or photodynamic therapy is a process where a fiber-optic cable is placed near the target tumor, and light is aimed precisely through it. When the beam hits the tumor cells, it kills them.
Malignancy	A cancerous tumor that can invade and destroy nearby tissue and spread to other parts of the body.
Metastasis	The spread of cancer from one part of the body to another. A tumor formed from cells that have spread is called a secondary tumor, a metastatic tumor, or a metastasis. The secondary tumor contains cells that are like those in the original (primary) tumor. The plural form of metastasis is metastases (meh-TAS-ta-seez).
Naturopathy	One who is trained to practice natural healing versus treating symptoms.
Natural Cleansing	Natural Cleansing or detoxification allowing the body to rid itself of toxins and poisons

NCI	National Cancer Institute established in 1937
Omega-3 Fatty Acids	Also known as alpha-linolenic acid, omega-3s are a fatty acid found in fish and vegetable oils. Omega-3s have protective functions in preventing the formation of blood clots, reducing the risk of coronary heart disease.
Organic	Chemical-free gardening, harvesting and manufacturing of foods
Parasitic (parasite)	An animal or a plant that lives on or in an organism of another species and gets nutrients from it. A complete parasite gets all of its nutrients from the host organism. For example, cancer cells that drain the energy
pH level	PH is Potential Hydrogen. It is the amount of hydrogen ions in a substance or solution. pH is measured on a logarithmic scale from 0 to 14. A higher number is more alkaline (cool and slow) and there is a greater potential for absorbing more hydrogen ions. Lower numbers indicate more acidity (fast and

hot) absorbing less hydrogen ions.

Food impacts the pH level in the body. The more acid foods we eat the faster more heated our body's operation eventually causing some type of malfunction. If we eat more alkaline foods, the body operates in a more cool slow state. A body with a pH of over 7 is alkaline and can maintain a better state of health.

Plant Protein	Protein from vegetables, grains and legumes.
Platelets	Fragments of cells that assist with blood clotting. Originate from bone marrow and is used in large quantities for cancer treatment.
Pure water	Unpolluted or filtered water
PSA Level	Prostate Specific Antigen level predicts the future growth of the prostate. A high level (over 4) could be a sign of abnormal cell growth.
Radiation	Treatment that employs high intensity X-rays to disable the reproduction of cancer cells.

Radical	Term used to describe some of the effects of conventional cancer treatments, which may extend life but permanently degrades the quality of life for the patient.
Radioisotopes	An unstable element that releases radiation as it breaks down. Radioisotopes can be used in imaging tests or as a treatment for cancer.
Staging	The extent of a cancer within the body. If the cancer has spread, the stage describes how far it has spread from the original site to other parts of the body.
Stem cells	A cell from which other types of cells can develop
Sweeper	Refers to the use of radiation therapy to ensure that the area where the malignancy is located, is treated at the microscopic level and no residual cancer cells remain.
Tempeh	Tempeh, is a chunky, tender soybean cake with a nutty flavor. Is sometimes blended with brown rice.

Surina Ann Jordan

Tinctures	A medication that is an alcoholic solution of an extract of a vegetable or animal substance or a chemical.
Ultrasound	A procedure in which high-energy sound waves (ultrasound) are bounced off internal tissues or organs and make echoes. The echoes form a picture of body tissues called a sonogram. Also called ultrasonography.

References:

www.nci.nih.gov/dictionary/
www.purelinatural.com/Glossary_t.html
www.soyfoods.com
www.biomedx.com/microscopes/rrintro/rr1.html
www.zoefoods.com/health_info/glossary.htm
www.colonhealth.net
www.news.bbc.co.uk/1/hi/health/1871474.stm
www.purelinatural.com/Glossary_n.htm
Page Rector, Linda, Health Healing, Healthy Healing Publications,
Pelton, R., Ph.D. and Lee Overholser, Ph.D. Alternative Cancer Therapy, Simon & Schuster, NY 1994.

Bibliography

Introduction

American Cancer Society, Cancer Facts & Figures, www.cancer.org, 2003.

Aihara, Herman. *Acid & Alkaline.* Oroville, CA: George Ohsawa Macrobiotic Foundation, 1986.

Castelman, Michael. *Blended Medicine.* USA: St. Martin's Press, 2000.

Howell, Edward. *Enzyme Nutrition.* Wayne, N.J.: Avery Publishing Group, 1985.

Fink, John M. *The Third Opinion.* Garden City, NY,: Avery Publishing Group Inc., 1992.

Ponder, Catherine. *The Dynamic Laws of Healing.* California: DeVorss & Company, 1966.

Surina Ann Jordan

Chapter One

Anatomy of a Cigarette,
www.thesite.org/info/drugs/smoking/anatomy_of_a_cigarette.html.

Yozwick, Chester. **Legal & Administrative Aspects of a Holistic Health Practice** (116).

Jensen, Bernard. *Tissue Cleansings Through Bowel Management.* California: Bernard Jensen Enterprises, 1981.

Lynes, Barry. The Healing of Cancer. Ontario, Canada: Marcus Books, 1990.

Burton Goldberg Group. *Alternative Medicine.* Washington: Future Medicine Publishing, Inc, 1994.

Page, Linda, *Healthy Healing.* Healthy Healing Publications, 1997.

Ponder, Catherine. *The Dynamic Laws of Healing.* California: DeVorss & Company, 1966.

Smokers Article www.healthscout.com

Bloom, B.L.; Asher, S. J.; and White, S. W. *Marital Disruption as a Stressor: A Review and Analysis.* Psychological Bulletin 85 no. 4 (1978): page 867-894.

Minding The Body: Stress. U of Wisconsin: Science Behind the News, www.whyfiles.org,

Chapter Two

Medical Encyclopedia. *Stages Of Cancer.* www.nlm.nih.gov

National Cancer Institute of Health Glossary of Terms, www.nci.gov

UK Cancer Information Service, Bone Marrow Article, www.cancerbacup.org.uk

bodyTemple News. Georgia: bodyTemple Maintenance, Winter 2002 edition.

Burton Goldberg Group. *Alternative Medicine.* Washington: Future Medicine Publishing, Inc, 1994.

Page, Linda. *Healthy Healing.* Healthy Healing Publications, 1997.

Chapter Three

Castleman, Michael. *Blended Medicine*. Pennsylvania: Rodale Book, 2000.

Newman, M. & Berkowitz, B. *How to Be Your Own Best Friend*. New York: Ballantine Books, 1971.

Peterson, Eugene. *The Message Bible*, CO: Navpress, 1993.

The New Analytical Bible. Iowa: World Bible Publishers, 1973.

Page, Linda, *Healthy Healing*, Healthy Healing Publications, 1997.

Balch, James G., Balch Phyllis S. New York: *Prescription for Nutritional Healing*, Avery, 1999.

Murray, Michael, N.D. *The Healing Power of Foods*. Prima Publishing, 1993.

Chapter Four

Salaman. Kennedy Maureen. *All Your Health Questions Answered Naturally*. California: MKS, Inc., 1998.

Peterson, Eugene. *The Message Bible*, CO: Navpress, 1993.

Page, Linda, *Healthy Healing*, Healthy Healing Publications, 1997.

Balch, James G., Balch Phyllis S. New York: *Prescription for Nutritional Healing*, Avery, 1999.

Murray, Michael, N.D. *The Healing Power of Foods.* Prima Publishing, 1993.

Appendix - Knowing your divine purpose.

First you must believe that there is a predestined map for your life, as it stated in Psalm 139. Before I had lived one day, my life was laid out. Take some time and consider the following questions. Your answers can be very helpful towards the discovery of your purpose:

1. What is it that I do that when I do it I lose all track of time?

2. What subjects do I find interesting and exciting when I learn more about them?

3. What productive thing comes to mind if I were to say, when I have more time or money I will do more of it?

4. What things come very natural for me?

5. What training or education have I had that I really enjoyed?

6. As impossible as it may seem, what is it that I really like to do?

If you are like many of us, you may answer these questions knowing that you are in a job or on a career path that is not fulfilling. One that does not fire your rockets but it does pay the bills and allows you to afford the creature comforts.

Many of us are afraid to admit that this situation exists in our lives. But the truth will set your free! And the denial could be killing you. It does not mean that you should turn in your resignation first thing in the morning. However, there are some questions you can begin asking God, letting him know that you're seeking knowledge and an understanding of your divine purpose. Once this is done, all of the answers to the above questions will begin to reveal a pattern that is unique to you. Some of them are stepping stones and some detours that might have taken you off track for a while.

Meditation:

Dear God, I have to know why you have granted me life and what is my work or purpose. I want to grab it and go with it. I intend to hold onto it as if my life depends on it because it really does. Thanks. In Jesus Name, Amen.

Surina Ann Jordan

Next Steps:

Journal your day. Read the bible and pray everyday

Remember: It is not what you do for God that is key. It is what God does through you.

About the Author

Surina Ann Jordan, M. S. was exposed to Alternative Medicine during a serious illness several years ago. Shortly after her illness her husband was diagnosed with cancer but today lives in complete health. She is a writer and publisher of *body*Temple News. This publication emphasizes increased health and nutrition through personal stewardship. Jordan is a member of the American Holistic Health Association (AHHA) and has been published in the AHHA electronic newsletter. She has a genuine concern for those who live in the bondage of poor health and seeks to liberate them through intervention and healthy living. She is the founder of the Eat to Live Network, a group that provides information and support to help people live conscious, healthy lifestyles. Jordan is a graduate of the Clayton College of Natural Health.

Printed in the United States
45334LVS00005B/382-516